MW01378221

Sunbeams of Love

SHERRI A. BYRUM

ISBN 978-1-0980-6519-5 (paperback)
ISBN 978-1-0980-6520-1 (digital)

Christian Faith Publishing, Inc.
832 Park Avenue
Meadville, PA 16335
www.christianfaithpublishing.com

Printed in the United States of America

Contents

It's My Father's World Part 1 7

It's My Father's World Part 2 8

My Voice...11

The Earth...13

Planet Earth 14

Echo Day 15

Life...16

The Beauty of Nature..17

Storms of Life..18

Sunshine on My Shoulders...19

Spring Is Here, Easter..20

Sunshine 21

Rain 22

Roses..23

The Blessed Curse, My Chain 24

Mountains and Valleys and Streams...................................27

Life Is a Blessing..29

Who Am I? 31

Ageless..32

Birthday Cheer..36

Be Happy 37

Beauty 1 38

Beauty 2...39

Footsteps..40

Worry Is a Web 42

AngerPart 1 43

AngerPart 2 44

War 45

God's Rescue Ladder 46

God's Fireman 47

God's Little Wonders 49

Doors 51

Love Never Fails 53

Let Love Rule Your Mind 54

Illuminate Me 56

God Is Love 57

Love Is in the Air 58

Love Is a Circle 59

My Dream Home 60

Heavenly Home 62

Wooden Park 64

Beach Days 65

Sand 67

Roses in Bloom 69

Cupid's Heart 71

Cupid's Arrow Continued 73

Lilacs 74

Songbirds 75

Butterfly 76

Hershey's Kisses 78

My Family Poems: A Time and a Season 80

Our Family Tree 82

Birds 83

My Mom 84

Brother Is a Friend 87

My Daughter, Jessica 88

My Christmas Baby, Heather 89

To My Girls 90

My Daughters 91

Family Tree 92

A Baby's Breath 93

My Grandchildren..94

My Granddaughter..95

My Grandson 96

Friends 97

Friendship 98

Christmas Joy..99

Christmas Cheer 100

New Year's Day..101

Tax Man..102

Death Is a Gateway 103

Peace 104

Retirement 105

Peace Be Still 106

This Day 107

Aged to Perfection..108

Honey Bear 109

The Watching 110

People Pleaser Versus God Pleaser..111

Heart..112

My Heart 113

Fathers, Love Your Sons..114

New Year's 2020 116

The Forest..117

God's Justice Versus Man's Injustice..119

Raindrops..120

It's My Father's World
Part 1

A little tear, oh, not this year,
Let's bring peace and calm round here.
A stream into a river, the river ran wild.
Her tears spilled into the ocean
Her wave of pain surged wild.
Into the Atlantic Ocean, it caused a tidal wave.
Uh-oh, maybe just another thought away.
So let's rejoice enjoy your day.
Help me to learn all of your holy ways,
To treat all people with respect
In God's kingdom, where we will be quite blessed.
May I learn to be more like you in everything I say and do.
May I choose to walk away from people who will not obey.

> "Guard me as the apple of the eye; hide me in the
> shadow of your wings" (Psalm 17: 8).

It's My Father's World
Part 2

Inside out, outside in,
You're on the inside; you're on the outside
You're inside out, outside in.
"Who's looking in?"
Now let's start over again. I feel like an alien.
Make sure the master wins…
Darkness on the outside,
Darkness on the inside,

Darkness looking in.
Light on the outside,
Light on the inside,
Light looking in,
You're inside out, outside in,
"Who's looking in?"
Let the master enter in,
Bring us safely home again.
Emotions on the outside, emotions on the inside.
You're inside out, outside in
Emotion's looking in,
Let God remove every sin,
While your emotion's are running thin,
Christ alone sees within…
"Who's looking in?"
Heart on the outside,
Heart on the inside,
Heart outside looking in,
Your inside out, outside in,
"Who's looking in?"
Let God dwell within
And mend your heart again…
Circle on the outside,
Circle on the inside,
Circle looking in,
You're inside out, outside in,
"Who's looking in?"
Let's all hold hands and pray again.
Let God blend our heart with his…
Sunshine on the outside,
Sunshine on the inside,
Sunshine looking in,
Your inside out, outside in "Who's looking in?"
Rays of light shining in,
Sunbeams of love filled to the brim,
"Who's looking in?"

Sunbeam's of love glistening through,
Skies filled with clouds
Erasing all the blue…
God's big eraser is following you.
Just as the weather disappears,
So does our sin. God made it clear.
Just as the sunshine's after the rain.
So God gives new life as he forgave.
Now shines a rainbow instead of a grave.
His promises are true to all he saves.
As we behold things we never knew…
Make sure you always run from sin.
Don't let Satan enslave from within.
Let God make you whole again.
God's new reveal "a brand-new you,"
From inside out, outside in,
Then back to love again…
"Who's looking in?"
God's smiling on his child again.

> "I removed his shoulder from the burden. His hands were freed from the baskets. You called in trouble, and I delivered you, I answered you in the secret place of thunder, I tested you at the waters of Meribah" (Psalm 81:6).

My Voice

As I lay down and reminisce about my day…
Flipping through the page's thoughts still in disarray…
Remembering how dramatic it all was one "echoed day…"
Woke up one early morning, nothing was the same.
Seems so long ago, yet seems like yesterday…
Seems like I was frozen scared to death to stay this way…
Like ice on top the ocean frozen in the bay.
One bibbidi-bobbidi-boo, I've lost my brain to you…
One poof with a wand and my voice forever gone.
Shouts on the street, shouts in air,
Shouts everywhere! Oh my god, I'm in my underwear…

Look at the people, look at the stares…
Brain waves on display. I now live in the air…
It's my voice. It's my sound.
Don't steal my freedom, where I was found.
I thought I was going down. Gone so fast, I thought I'd drowned…
Remember ground zero and how far we've come…
God let us out no need to run.
Landed in your living room, flying swiftly on a broom.
Oh no, that's not me. It's Satan's boo crew…
All his demons lined up like little toy soldiers ready for battle.
Each has a name, part of the cursor.
Jumping in my brain waves, just like riding a toy train.
Always trying to gain speed, trying to be my master.
Always trying to blast her…God simply says, "thoughts aren't your master".

> "Blessed are the peace makers, for they shall be called the children of God" (Matthew 5:9).

> "Do not strive with a man without a cause if he has done you no harm" (Proverbs 3:30).

The Earth

I walk outside and see the trees,
Feel the breeze, the autumn leaves.
I see you in your baby's eyes while searching thoughts,
Through beautiful blue skies…
This means New Year's Eve's almost here.
I've learned to smile at loss this year.
Happiness is a smile away, turning into sunshine.
Takes away the gray. I'm learning new beauty in everything.
God's mercy is new for the echo today.
So enjoy the journey that God's thrown your way.
Keep your head up, be humble, and pray.
Remember to thank God for each and every day.

> "A man's mind plans his way, but the Lord directs his steps" (Proverbs 16:9).

> "Oh, taste and see that the Lord is good, blessed is the man who trusts in him" (Psalm 34:8).

Planet Earth

I'm sitting on the planet, dangling my feet.
Playing with the stars, connect them with my feet.
Strolling on the rainbows, colors burst in air.
Butterflies are dancing to a new tune everywhere.
Sun is shining brightly rays oh so bright and fair.
While the seagulls are soaring way up in the air,
Beautiful in flight watch the fireflies fight,
Something becomes quite clear,
I feel real peace over here.
God's beauty is amazing, and I began a praising,
The one who made it all who answers all my calls,
Tears down all my walls, and always knows it all.

> "I have made a covenant with my chosen. I have sworn to my Servant David your seed I will establish forever, and build up Your throne to all generations" (Psalm 89:3).

Echo Day

I'm not sure which way to run, been so long since I had fun.
I long to lay out in the sun. It's peaceful in the morning bliss.
It warms my skin, brightens my day. I see the sun a fiery red ball,
Setting in the east, and that's not all.
The good news is we're all still here through all the tragedies this year.
Broken bones will mend and heal, so make sure you live real this year.
Live out in love your golden years. Breathe in breath out.
Live in, live out, living on the inside, living on the outside,
Living inside out.

> "Behold this is the joy of his way, and out of the
> earth others will grow. God will not cast away the
> blameless, nor will he uphold the evildoers. Till
> he yet fill your mouth with laughing and your
> lips with rejoicing. Those who hate you will be
> clothed in shame, and the dwelling place of the
> wicked will come to nothing" (Job 8:19–22).

Life

Just a prayer at the end of my day
Turn the storms into another day…
I love to sing, I love to shout
Through the rough spots, there is no doubt,
Through the wind and through the rain,
Through the snow then start over again.
She's coming back to life again with the pain
In my vein, I feel it running through again.
I think she's done it again, poison in, poison out.
She's trying to take my life no doubt.
"Move away, move away," watching my back every day,
I can't take much more, or I will be on the floor,
As God gently states, "My power is great,"
You'll live and not die, beyond all you'll rise…

> "He that dwelleth in the secret place of the most
> high will abide under the shadow of the almighty"
> (Psalm 91:1).

The Beauty of Nature

I woke up this morning in awe of what God has done.
A beautiful morning miracle follows from tree to tree.
Birds, bees, and butterflies now following me.
The beauty of earth now possessing me.
Singing another beautiful song, I feel the power of love.
I love to watch the deer walking inside the park.
They're all whispering so sweetly; God lives within your heart.
He never let me down or looked the other way, never ever a frown,
Only love glowing from his face.
That's real love I'm hooked. I'll have it no other way.
The beauty of God's reveal, using Mother Nature to heal.
Helping me on my way while many others betrayed.
God says your the best, just don't look down today.
Don't look the other way. When you meet the real God,
You'll never run away.

> "For I know the thoughts that I think towards
> you saith thy God. Thoughts of peace, not of evil
> to give you an expected end" (Jeremiah 29:11).

Storms of Life

So when you feel worn down by life,
Sailing from storm to storm, tattered, torn, weather beaten, forlorn.
Look to the master of the seas. Truth of the matter is he will never leave.
When you feel the gloomiest, he'll rise up from the sea.
He'll help you conquer every test.
He'll guide both you and me.
Never let go of his hand don't look back to see sea monster reappear.
Jesus lifted up his hand, and calmed the screaming sea.
And calmed the screaming sea.
Men, put your hands back down now. Her eyes are glued on me.
She needs a Christian man who loves her unconditionally.
A man who's more like me.
I'm all she ever really needs.
There's safety staying with your guide. He knows the water's better
than I
To turbulence I am blind. Keep your eye on the guide.
Follow in unison. Let the Lord lead. Safety in numbers as our Savior
pleads
"Listen to me. We'll ride out the sea. Sea billows almost over. Another
win for thee."

> "Jesus Christ the same yesterday, today, and for-
> ever" (Hebrews 13:8).

Sunshine on My Shoulders

As the sun rises, we know warmth is near.
A beautiful day that brings my heart cheer.
See the sunset's majestic in beauty,
Fluorescent colors on canvas descending in beauty…
Watching the gases dissipate just as darkness follows night.
Evaporating in beautiful flight at the bay into the night.
It's beautiful to watch the moonlight reappear.
While the sunlight disappears into thin air,
The other side of the earth shouts with cheers.
It's our time to wake up over here; a new day has appeared.

> "Jesus Christ the same yesterday, today, and forever" (Hebrews 13:8).

Spring Is Here
Easter

Spring is here. Rejoice this year.
I've never tasted a sweeter tear.
Beautiful blossoming flowers, gorgeous everywhere.
Jesus has resurrected. New life is here to share.
Feel God's spirit floating in the air…feel it everywhere.
My heart is resurrected; my new cross I share.
I'm feeling real things this year, beautiful to hear.

> "A new heart I will give you, and a new spirit I
> will put within you; and I will remove from your
> body the heart of stone, and give you a heart of
> flesh" (Ezekiel 36:26).

Sunshine

It's very repetitious circular beauty here.
God's morning miracle has arrived with love, my dear.
With an uncanny resemblance of sunshine in the air,
The blueprint finally finished, handle with tender care.
Masterpiece in the making, Jesus was always there.

> "The Lord make his face shine upon you, and
> bless his people with peace" (Psalms).

Rain

Every pitter patter and every titter tatter.
Raindrops falling down faster, faster, faster.
We haven't seen the sun for years, it seems.
Like drops in the ocean, tears finally seized.
Crystallized through pain, seared like sugarcane.
Heart melted faster from the pain turned into rain.
Look to your maker, he will lead you home.
At dawn, in a boat, yelling, "Breaker, breaker!
Put the phone down and yell for your maker."

"Wait for the Lord, be strong and take heart.
Wait I say on the Lord" (Psalm 27:14).

Roses

Roses are red, violets are blue.
Know that my heart is always with you.
Sings for you, shouts for you, but most of all, wholly adores you.
Through the wind, through the rain,
Hearts are mending beautifully all over again.

> "If we love one another, God dwells deeply within us, and his love becomes complete in us" (1 John 4:11).

"Perfect love."

The Blessed Curse My Chain

I'd like to share my story of how I went on air. One morning, I woke to find my sweet spirit there.

Life quickly became a nightmare because everyone was there. So I'd like to share my day from morning until noon. I feel betrayed all day with people talking about everything I do.

It starts with the DJ hosts, and then the beast arrives. He likes my attention the most. The beast starts to hover. He likes to listen to the mother shutter.

He's grouchy and defiant, noisy and rude.

Then he starts to touch and bother and break all the golden rules.

Causes heat as if it doesn't bother. Might knock me over in the shower with his evil power.

Causes demons to dance in my head. Then I go to work and handle all his friends.

Sometimes it's hard to handle this attachment to my body. It's unbelievable. We're all alittle frightened. Shhh… show no fear. You might scare everybody.

This kind of crime, who could have thought. I hope he isn't staying. My thoughts changed very rapidly. From the curse the beast did place. He's angry and controlling. His demons will not give me my free space. I feel like every day is a relay race.

My children started to wonder where their mom went to.

I started cursing daily just to make it through.

Forgetting about prayer and all things I'd been taught. It all went out the window as each day people started to taunt.

Slander, ridicule, disrespect became the norm.

People in my business whom I don't adore.

Thank God for other people who try to lift me up. Radio hosts who speak kind words and build my spirit up.

It's dramatic for all of us every day. None of us had a choice in the beast's baseball game.

My children are now afraid of the one who made their life, tucked them in at night, and the stories that she read.

Now they think she's a little crazy because she lives inside her head. I try to focus on what I'm doing, but I'm always listening to the noise in the backdrop. Looking people's approval of me.

Spending all day wondering what other people think made this moment a nightmare, a new catastrophe. As I step into unfamiliar ground with God holding my hand, I'm trying to find my peace inside of "Echo land." God has assured me it's just another part of his plan. He will never harm me; other people can. I still have some fears about what I'm really doing here.

Then I finally realized God is in control. I guess I really wanted God to remove the curse, instead of all the miracles he placed on the earth.

Although there very beautiful, I'm scared of Mother Earth. I can't put into words all that God has done. I was thrown into the dark abyss where I was alone, and so I thought I need to go home. With the public watching, I began to fall. I kept running into an invisible wall. Blow by blow, it hits harder every day. I had to call on God many times a day.

He made me in his image. He calls "the stars" by name. God's spirit comforts beautifully, and now I'm fully grown. Now I'm the one he calls me to be. I'm one of his own. Now I can handle this chain tied to me. Realizing all the while, God used it to heal me. Now I am free. Christ resides inside of me.

There is no storm hard enough. There is no sea rough enough. That's God's weather guard isn't enough.

> "I will be God throughout your lifetime, until your hair is white with age. I made you, and I will care for you. I will carry you along and save you" (Isaiah 46:4).

Mountains and Valleys and Streams

I walked up to the mountain, and I was feeling scared. As much as I like walking, I thought I saw a bear. I didn't think I could make it into the trees. So I stopped for a needed reprieve. Then I decided to follow the stream. I put on my backpack and felt a sudden squeeze. Then I saw the face of Jesus, and he said, "It's getting too heavy, I will carry it for thee." So I started on my journey through the Appalachian breeze. It's a little chilly, "Can I have my jacket please?" Now I see a deer walking alongside me in the stream. Also there are eagles hovering all around me. Take out your camera. Take many pictures please. Make sure you see the beautiful autumn leaves that Daddy made for me to see. I'm lost in the forest. So walk a little farther down the stream. The momma bear and her cubs are making a new scene. Swatting at the fish, can I have one please before I leave? Don't get to close; she may decide to fillet me.

God looking over and said, "Have no fear Jesus is near". Go a little farther down the stream. Momma duckling protecting babies swimming in the stream, all her quacking right beside me. Now I'm ready for some tea. Sit down at the picnic table that's right beside me. A little relaxation and rest time. Time to just be me. Soon I'll walk the canyon and behold God's majesty. Take lots of pictures. Enjoy God's beauty with glee. So you will never forget where God has brought thee. God winked at me, and I winked back. I see his smile through the trees. He has my backpack. Not your time to leave. Don't look back. You need to reach the mountaintop. Just hurry. Let's scurry through the twisting and turning. Don't be alarmed as you go on God's journey. Enjoy each second of the journey. As you look around, you see God's smile. Go ahead and linger for a while. It's an adventure more wonders to behold. Can't wait to see what the rest of the mountain holds.

> "You are more glorious and excellent than the mountains of prey" (Psalm 76:4).

Life Is a Blessing

I never tasted a sweeter year. My tree is in full bloom this year. Now
  I have spices, and I cheer.
No new burdens and needless cares.
Trees are beautiful everywhere. The clouds are moving quickly way
  up in the air.
They look like cotton candy, pink and blue sugarcane for all to share.
Beauty on the horizon stars shooting everywhere.
Lightening flashing in the sky, causing tears in my eyes. Beautiful and
  bold watch God's majesty unfold. I hear the creator say, "Look
  ahead and keep pressing on.
No matter the season, don't be forlorn."
It's all a part of a beautiful plan delivered from the master's hands.
It may not be the route I'd choose, but with God as our guide, we
  cannot lose.
If we fall, we rise again. God is your king and your best friend.
As I kneel down and pray today…
To the God who sends the rain, I pray he sends new love my way.
Find joy in pain,
Smile through the rain,
Love through the pain,
Pray to endure all chains
Pray without ceasing,
While you drive through each season.
Guide me for your grander reason.
Keep me safe from all treason.

"Trust in the Lord with all your heart lean not unto your own understanding, in all your ways acknowledge him, and he shall direct your path" (Proverbs 3:1).

"Everyone born of God overcomes the world" (1 John 5:4).

Who Am I?

A new life is given; its here to stay.
Be like a butterfly. Soon fly away.
Spread your wings far,
Write your name in the stars.
God gave me new freedom,
Share it with all kingdoms.
Did you ever wonder what the world would be?
Without a sound in the background,
A sounds that's just like me?
Or another sound, a sound you cannot see.
Oh my goodness, who could it possibly be?
Uh-oh, I think it's always been me.
Did you ever wonder how her curls should be?
What she really looks like all that you can't see.
Did you ever consider she has the most beautiful heart?
Who could this woman be as precious as can be?
Is she the one messing with idolatry?
Tick, tick, tock, times run out on the clock.
I think we need to meet, old age befalling me.
Did you ever wonder why it has to be?
Always war between you and me.
If I give utterance to the king,
I think it's really about destiny.

> "Yea I have loved thee with an everlasting love: Therefore, with loving kindness I have drawn thee" (Jeremiah 31:3).

Ageless

Time marches on. It's taking me hostage.

A prisoner of war you cannot stop it.

A windowless prison. "Uh-oh," another new year,

A gun at your side, a field of gray hairs.

Colonel says, "Move forward," with a gun in my back.

"We're going outside. There's gonna be another attack."

I drop to my knees. He's making me move farther.

My stomach can't handle the twisting and turning.

A battle zone next to my door. Don't be afraid. God's coming to settle the score.

God's here to save and won't stop at any age.

So run, run, run away, run faster every day.

Always stay behind the lines, enemies waiting to crucify. It's a new life. You're not going to the grave.

Much, much grace for every day. So the colonel shouts move and points to me again.

God yells down, "He's not your master."

Another war tactic they try to squeeze…all the while adding more poison in me.

More information we need from you please, so I open a book, but I can no longer see.

All of the words that God gave to me, all of the words I did retrieve. While I was waiting all the while to be freed, I died again. Sir, let me go please.

Afraid to walk away and can no longer run…

I prayed to God to send his son. I need a rescue and a save.

They stole me, and I won't cave. All the while fighting for privacy, they kept ignoring all my pleas. My father graciously said, "Let her go please, she wants to be free and continue worshipping me." The war was over long ago. She never stopped to grieve.

Meanwhile, grim reaper caught up with me. I looked in the mirror. Oh, what did I see? A brand new woman inside my ear. She doesn't look the same as she did before, but she's gonna escape right though her new door. Don't try to stop her troops marching again. Shhh…

The shock of the sound wakes all the men.

They're stirring around. I feel scared again.

They're getting closer. They think they're gonna win.

The crowd's yelling, "Crucify her, crucify her!"

God yells down back up now. I want you to win. You can't see what I can see.

"Just please trust me," Jesus said. "I'm your ally. I'm your win. My war tactics don't include sin. While on your knees, remember to pray for God to keep all enemies away."

One by one, the troops retrieve. Finally, the slave is freed.

She fell in love with the new me.

Angels never disgraced, more grace. Angels everywhere, angels in the air, angels on the ground, angels sitting in the dust, angels in the sound. This angel will rebound. Angels carried her to higher ground. When I was down, thought I would never be found.

Angels flapped their wings as soon as they heard my sound. They fly right down, spin in my ear, whispering new songs to sing this year with shouts of cheer…

Wave goodbye as they leave, angels really never grieve. They still fly at my side, didn't know they're just my guide. Catch a glimpse of them midair, angels' dust is everywhere.

Now write it down, all that you've seen its jubilant and its free.

What a God he is to me. My defendant through the war. Every detail he knew the score. Not a rock unturned where he leads me to higher ground where I meet thee.

See me upright. You're not alone here.

I'm Michael, your prince, be of good cheer. God sent me to you to undo the blue…God's assured me he wants me to guide you.

Don't be upset. I know he's unruly. God did make him; he's the perfect fit for me.

Whatever it takes for what ails you, God doesn't make mistakes. Please let him bless you...

Don't be scared. He cannot rule you. It's just the way God wants to renew you.

So let the potter mold the clay into a vessel that cannot break.

It cannot shatter or shake. (Oh no, another earthquake!) It stands firm in the midst of the storm.

It calls on Jesus to fulfill his season. It ignores all treason. It can only make better a new model than the one she thought she did break.

Let the angels walk you through your next door to.

The artillery needed for God's beautiful new war.

God's wrath is past over. All that's been done, innocent blood was shed.

Battles already fought and won. Through the blood of Jesus, he's the only holy one...

Angels disgraced, no angels give grace,

Angels about-face,

Angels for war, no angels for more,

Angels untied prisoner of war,

Now she's really free to soar.

Angels came to settle the score.

Make sure you're happy and healthy once more.

So I will follow and carry on teaching God's rules for his own. We follow through till we get home, where a mansion we will own. There are benefits for his own. To obey God's laws brings blessings untold. So with the microphone in his hand, just a part of a beautiful plan. A tool he made to finish his plan. If we ask, we shall receive all of the blessings he has for me. A new creation is waiting to behold your Father's majesty.

> "Therefore, if the son makes you free, you shall
> be free indeed" (John 8:36).

Birthday Cheer

Happy, happy birthday!
Made me merriest this year.
Born on Christmas day,
How we were blessed with cheer.
A little love was given a very special gift.
Blanketed in snowdrifts,
Angels were our guests.

> "Happy are those who live in your house, Ever singing your praise" (Psalm 84:4).

Be Happy

Happy hopped up in my head, said he came to cheer me up, said he brought a friend. Happy put on some music to praise and worship then.

So we hopped over to dance for a while with Happy in the den. Happy said, "You need to smile and make yourself some friends." Happy hopped in my garden, said something needs to mend.

Happy takes out the bitter roots and lets new blossoms win. Don't stay sad and lonely with grim reaper on his way.

Happy introduced me to a special way.

Dealing with my anger, don't let it rule your day.

Don't let anger rear his head instead try to bend.

Put a smile back on your face, no regrets today,

Wash all wrath away,

Enjoy a better way,

Don't make Happy run away,

Happy wants to stay…

Hippitty, hoppity, Happy…

> "Cast all your care upon him, for he careth for you" (1 Peter 5:7).

Beauty 1

Beauty from within, beauty from without,
Beauty on the outside, beauty looking in,
People look on the outside. God only looks within.
Let him free the chains holding you only in.
Beauty in the sunshine, beauty in the rain,
Let God's love shine in and heal your heart today.
As we all know, God's love will save the day!

> "For god so loved the world that he gave his only
> begotten son that Whosoever believeth in him shall
> not perish, but have everlasting life" (John 3:16).

Beauty 2

Beauty is ageless, perfected in time, just like a fine wine when you dine.

Love is ageless, perfect beauty here. If you stare to long, you might start to tear.

As you see little wrinkles starting to appear, just remember this when you look into the mirror.

You haven't changed at all. Are things becoming clearer?

Your beauty resides within, so put your heart into your mirror.

Now let's play your heartstring. Is it becoming clearer?

Beauty comes from inside. Jesus is the healer.

> "When Jesus saw him lying there he knew he had been in that condition along time, he Said to him, 'wilt thou be made whole?'" (John 5:6).

Footsteps

I hear his footsteps on the stairs.
I see his footprints as I stare.
I run back and forth forever scared.
I see his silhouette on my wall.
I'm terrorized by the monster coming down the hall.
He circles my room every day.
Can't seem to keep the monster at bay.
Such a strange twist of fate. Forever feel his hate.
Like a boxing match wants to seize my brain.
Makes tears flow down like the rains.
Is it my real life or his delusion I fear?
Am I stuck in my bed or is it all in my head?
Can't move away, so I stay frozen from the monster at the bay.

He's on his way to take me away.
I'm frozen now from the scare.
Don't leave your body; he's almost there.
Feel him move under the blanket.
Uh-oh, he's stolen all that's sacred.
The frozen waters are melting fast.
Frozen icicles dripping into puddles on the grass.
I feel I may drown as God melts my heart. All walls are down.
Stay in your mind, always rebound.
Left me lifeless on the floor, cold and naked like before.
The same they stole from child to woman.
All I abhor and deplore.
Pain gone forevermore, just some stains left to tame,
As you grew up always the same.
Feeling unsafe, feeling unworthy,
Always distrust, always hurting.
Then God entered in, made me rise to life again.
Made a brand-new heart buffed out all the scars.

> "There is no fear in love; perfect love casteth out
> fear" (1 John 4:18).

Worry Is a Web

Today worry came to meet me rocking in a chair.
Brought discontentment with him and confusion to the air.
Worry is a web we so quickly weave…
So soon become entangled in the middle of the web until we cannot
leave.
He started in the morning, throwing accusations in the air,
Rocking back and forth frantically, just another red flare.
Just before you know it, I thought my life's all unfair.
Listen to his lies, tie me back to the chair that was never fair.
So I have to ask worry and discontentment to please leave because
God knows and cares.
I was happy in my rocking chair before worry came to greet me, and
I offered him a chair.
We rocked hard together, thought it might be fair.
God knows it didn't get me anywhere.
So when you start your day,
Make sure you pray,
Kick all discontentment away.
Focus on today,
Choose to love yourself always…
And a brand-new day.

"The prayer of the righteous is powerful and effective" (James 5:16).

Anger
Part 1

It's a little crazy when anger comes to meet me, changes my mood in an instant, and not very discreetly.

Feel it rise up inside where it wants to reside (mind, body, and soul).

Wants to yell and scream and conquer all my dreams...

Has to have its way. It's selfish, proud, and rude, always loves starting a tude.

It's greedy when I'm feeling needy. It's a mirrored reflection of my heart attitude.

"What is the tune you wanna play? Do you wanna shout and scream at me today?

Do you feel the need to get up and run away?

Take a look inside, see what song you play.

Maybe it's time to change the chorus that you play...

Same tune playing every single day.

Time to get up now. It's time to walk away. Put on a new tune and play it throughout the day. Tell anger he can no longer stay. Tell yourself you're wonderful as you go throughout the day. Give God your anger and choose to walk away. God doesn't make mistakes. So let us kneel down and pray.

"Let me hear joy and gladness" (Psalm 51:8).

Anger
Part 2

Today anger pushed and pulled, tied me with a rope to a chair, sent up a red flare.

Wanted me to scream and shout while no one was around.

Wants me to be bitter and place blame everywhere. This road leads to danger. I'm scared to drive down there. It could send you sailing to places unaware. If you look in the rearview mirror, you might get a scare. Anger wants to arrest, keep you hostage many years. If you don't escape it, prison bars will clank for years. There's no need to keep yourself in there.

> If the anger of a ruler rises against you don't leave
> your post.

War

The aftermath of war is here.
I can still see and hear.
Sounds of solace still the air, dead bodies everywhere.
I hope war never threatens again. God's wrath delivered.
Many hearts still need to mend.
The fury thrown here by God; they shouldn't worship other gods.
They shouldn't worship idols just because…
A nation divided, terror rushes in.
You can't be attacked without when you were attacked within.
United we stand, "the American team" to the really unbelief,
Waiting on God to deliver from regime.
In the aftermath of my betrayal, I find myself to be Cain, not Abel.
Follow God through the scam to find a line drawn in the sand.
He's been here since the world began,
Gently leading us home again.

> "Wisdom has built her house, she has set up her
> seven pillars. She has slaughtered her beasts…she
> has also set her table" (Proverbs 9:1–2).

God's Rescue Ladder

Angel's unaware, angels everywhere, in my memory rendezvous,
there's a special spiral staircase descending from heaven to you...
Where angels come to greet me and use it to pass through.
Descending up and down the stairs from heaven to my room.
Angels descending with light from above shining down on me in love.
It's where I meet my bodyguard protector of his worth.
Angels visiting me in my dreams and telling me I have the same
worth...
As all the treasures we've accumulated here on earth.
God was with me and knew my name before my birth.
Before my guardian angel ascends back up the stairs,
He sends me one more little prayer.
He sprinkles angel dust all over my hair. Wake up now, child, there's
no time left to spare.
I'm staying in your memory rendezvous; I leave God's peace with
you there.
You can always visit again before I float back up the stairs. Wake up
now, there are feathers floating everywhere.

"The name of the Lord is a strong tower. The
righteous run to it and are safe" (Proverbs 18:10).

God's Fireman

When I got home and walked up to my door,
I saw flames shooting all around the floor.
I touched the doorknob, and it scorched my hand.
I jumped up afraid to say,
"Where is God in this crazy plan?"
Is there no end of suffering for his friend?
Then I look over, and I see God's hand still in the plan.
His scars are visible; he died for our land.
He opened the door, and I see marred hands reaching for me with
    the palm of his hand.
Don't be afraid to walk through the flame. It cannot hurt you. The
    heat it will melt, mend, and bend.
Don't linger too long. The flames look so scary, but I was there all
    along, even when it was dreary.
Marching down the street, fire hose in his hands, sounding more like
    a band.
Waltz's up my lane, wants to extinguish all the flames.
Opens up the door, tells me to holler, "Lord." I said I already did.
    God's here to save the girl.
One by one, up the ladder to save the girl. That's what matters.
Throw a rope through the window, pull her out. The wolves are
    howling. Surrounded the ladder at the base, now a new pack of
    wolves in my face…
The cross in the fire,
God's love in the flame,
Walk away from the ashes,
And start over again…
God did grieve on the cross,
So there's no need to bleed.

We heed the good shepherd.

In every tragedy bestows grace to get all sheep home free...

When you pass through the waters, I will be with you; and through the rivers, they shall not overflow you. When you walk through the fire, you shall not be burned nor shall the flame scorch you. (Isaiah 43:2)

God's Little Wonders

The clouds today were beautiful rays…
Pinks, blues, and yellows too.
Set like a stage, God's platform displayed
Where I kneel to worship you…
God has a special gift waiting for you there.
It comes from his spirit down through the air.
While waiting for more beauty to view,
A new stage is set, one made brand-new.
I hear God's microphone call out to you,
So I turn around and smile at the ground,
And point, "I thought God was talking to you?"
I planned this show before time began.
Now you know I'm your best friend.
The stage is set. Please don't relent!
Please don't cry. It's not the end.
Just get up and adlib again…
Don't be scared. I'm always near.
God winked at me today, and I winked back.
He's the one who always has your back.
No time to sleep, no time to rest, no time for regrets.
Relentless new pursuit beautiful show next.
The encore coming straight from my heart.
Beautiful fireworks, it's a new start.
I'll take you further than you ever thought.
My father carried me here on angel's wings filled with chatter.
Where I found myself again and realized that all of me really matters.
God wouldn't let me down with the weight from the sound.
To carry, so he carried it for me.
To show God's light for all the world to see

To show he's in control of history.
He wanted me to share all that I see. Every stage God set perfectly.
God's writing in the sky beautiful messages
On how to survive his grandest finale.

> "Every good and perfect gift is from above coming down from the Father of lights" (James 1:7).

Doors

I see a door. It's in my way. I can't get through. All I see is rain.

The wind is howling, boisterous today.

The fog is dense. Can't make my way.

I see another door. It's in my way. A wolf is howling, scared me away. The stairs are old, and they may cave. Which way to go? Ask God and pray.

Which door to take to make my way? I enter one and start to pray, Dear God, can you please stop the rain.

The water resides, so I walk up to the window pane.

Get a little closer, I see myself inside in the rain, in the pain.

God looked at me and said, "What would you like to change? Look in the other door, and you decide your fate."

I walk through the yard, and the wolf runs my way.

He's ready to attack needs to protect his family.

I put up my arm, hoping he would leave, instead he jumped up and bit me extensively, and I started to bleed. I looked up and asked God, why he didn't see all that was gonna happen to me. Why he didn't protect me?

God looked at me and rolled up his sleeve. The scars you have weren't from me. I'm the one who never leaves. You need to know all you can be. You'll never find me hiding behind the trees.

Now which door shall it be? Hurry up before you can no longer see.

I want you to have all that I promised thee.

Follow closely, sit on my knee, my goal is never to harm thee.

I can't choose for thee. You must decide what you should be.

Use all that talents I've given thee. If I tell you what's better, you'll run the other way I see.

So make a move, and I'll protect thee. Open another door, I will see no more grief. I'll never leave you. You're chained to me.

You decide who you should be. I'll carry you through.
I wanna be with thee.

> "Behold I stand at the door and knock if any man hear my voice and open the door I will come in" (Revelation 3:20).

> "I am the door if anyone enters by me, he shall be saved, and will go in and out and find pasture. The thief does not come except to steal, rob, and destroy" (John 10:9–10).

Love Never Fails

Perfect love casts out fear
Have no fear when Jesus is near.
Held my hand through the years.
Brushed away all my tears. Never left me alone over here.
Justified all my fears.
Brings peace inside where I reside.
Brings hope and health back to my mind.
At the name of Jesus, Satan has to flee
And cease from bothering me.
Don't forget to say his name.
He's the one who breaks all chains.
Make sure you give glory to his name.
His majesty will always reign.

> "My peace I give you, not as the world gives give
> I to you. Do not let your heart's be troubled, and
> do not be afraid" (John 14:27).

Let Love Rule Your Mind

Protect your heart, protect your mind.
Let your conscience be your guide.
Keep your Bible by your side.
For peace and harmony, you must strive.
Remember you are Christ's bride.
Love without, love within,
Share it with all people because it always wins,
Then circles back to you again.
Perfect love, perfect peace,
Makes all the striving cease.
Perfect love casts out fear,
Jesus makes it very clear.
Joy within, joy without,
May you choose joyous living
And remove any doubts.
Something you can't live without…
Joy in your heart, joy on your face,
Make sure you keep yourself in a safe place.
Pruning within, pruning without,
Let water run in your garden,
Making it beautiful again,
Standing grandest in full bloom,
God's handiwork sent straight to you,
Flows from each branch for you,
Beautiful colors all in full bloom.
Love, joy, peace, blooming from the kind things you do.
Now your garden is the best standing grander than the rest.
Roses sprouting out like the water spout,
And spewing across the grounds.

As your heart heals like the waterspout,
Tip it over and let love pour out.
Let each bloom inside your heart make a beautiful fire start.
God's not interested in defeat; he wants a peaceful place for you to
    rest your feet.
Fill your heart with lots of rest.
What you put inside, make sure it's the best.
Don't listen to Satan's lies.
Make sure you pass all God's tests.
He only keeps the best.
Just like the rose blush you will rebloom.
Enjoy the new season Christ's given you.

> "A merry heart doeth good like a medicine but a
> broken spirit will dry the bones" (Proverbs).

Illuminate Me

Illuminate me in your presence,
Illuminate me in your peace.
How I feel in your presence is "oh so sweet."
Let it permeate me. I never wanna leave.
I see the light, it's "oh so bright," enter in where we need no night.
Saturated in God's love, his presence descending on me from above.
Peace flows through me like a river, flowing freely from the giver.
Permeated in his love, a beautiful gift from above,
Where I'm safe and feel such love.
I stay there and linger awhile where there's no time and no sound.
Illuminate your world again, bring us together, make us reblend.
Hold us sweetly in your hands, send us what we need to lead.
Make us greater. God, take the lead.
Illuminate our face to yours. Make us holy. This year's yours.
May I forever offer forgiveness and never settle scores.
So you can relent of war…never retaliate, leave all hate.

> "Now return to the lord your God for he is gracious
> and compassionate, slow to anger, abounding in
> lovingkindness, and relenting of evil" (Joel 2:13).

God Is Love

Every day I rise, tumult fills the air.
Then I read God's Word, and something becomes quite clear.
This is a time of judgement, and we all are very scared.
God is a god of mercy, and so we're all still living here.

> "The lord is high above the nations, and his glory above the heavens…who is like the Lord our God? who dwelleth on high, who humbleth Himself to behold the things that are in heaven, and the earth" (Psalm 113:4–6).

> "To everything there is a season and a time to every purpose to under heaven" (Ecclesiastes 3:1).

Love Is in the Air

Love is like a circle spinning in the air.
Round and round, it goes many tears it bears,
Because its never ending won't leave you alone on air.
Would soar right beside you and wipe away your tears.
Fighting off the enemies whose mission is very clear,
One by one as they appear, make sure you stand clear.
Demons on the run, afraid of what they've done,
Still trying to punish the good one, still think they've won,
Mission undone, God's battlefield is grand. He's the greatest man.
He's the only king who would gladly give a ring.
With it wed his bride church of God at his side.
As he tests and tries, he never leaves their side.
Inside booms and threats, outside car trouble on the rise.
Demons everywhere blasting in my ear, feel them in the air,
Testing everywhere, they're dancing with the devil, I hear there
Joyous cheers bragging on another evil year.
I met Satan's son, but I have angels unaware
To guide me everywhere.
God's son is still alive and with me for my journey in the air.

> "The lord is my shepherd I shall not want he maketh me to lie Down in green pastures he leadeth me beside the still waters" (Psalm 23:1).

Love Is a Circle

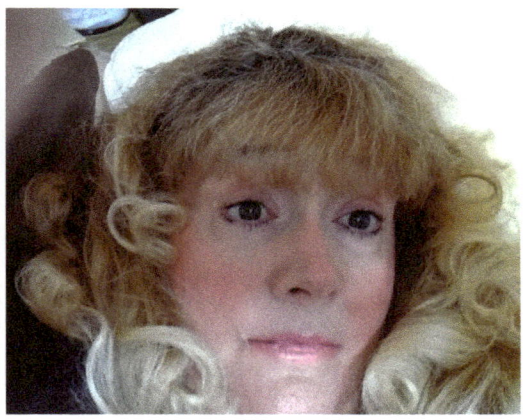

Love is a circle; it never really ends.
It spins and spins and spins until new love it mends.
In a circular motion, back and forth, it bends.
Through the twists and turns then back to love again.
The earth is a circle on which its axis spins,
All placed by the creator until the perfect blend.
Put your hand in God's; he will gently lead you home
To a place where tears one day will all be gone.

> "Yea I have loved thee with an everlasting love,
> therefore with lovingkindness have I drawn thee"
> (Jeremiah 31:3).

> "And we know that all things work together
> for good to them that love God, and are called
> according to his purpose" (Romans 8:28).

My Dream Home

Look into her eyes, they lead you to her heart.
The chain they linked to her cannot be broke apart,
Instead its breaking her only heart.
Leads to a beautiful pathway, a long and bumpy road.
It twists into her garden, a safe and beautiful home,
Where she'll never ever be alone.
Walk up in the driveway, it's along dirt road,
To her own safe haven where God is on the throne.
A rocker on the porch, grandchild on my knee,
Picket fence wrapped around the trees.
Doggies in the yard, barking loud as loud can be,
All her flowers blooming (oh, there everywhere)
Blowing in the breeze, pollens everywhere,
Humming birds enjoy the air, butterflies dancing there.
Fireflies in the air.
Birds are flying tree to tree, rainbow in the sky for me.
Welcome to my dream home! Are you scared of me?
Its grand as grand can be.
Would you like to stop in and share a pot of tea with me?
Would you love to share some sacred thoughts of me?
Maybe you should stop and pray awhile with me.
It's a wonderful place to be…wonderful home to see.
Please come in and greet me because you're welcome here.
Angels are our special guest, "Make us rest, make us rest."
It was all one grand test.

> "Behold this is the joy of his way, and out of the
> earth others will grow. Behold God will not cast
> away the blameless, nor will he uphold the evil

doers, till he yet fill your mouth with laughing and your lips with rejoicing those who hate you will be clothed in shame, and the dwelling place of the wicked will come to nothing" (Job 8:19–22).

Heavenly Home

God's dinner party, please don't be late.
He illuminates, permeates, takes away all the hate.
Sit at my feet, enter through the gate.
It's where never-ending peace saturates.
Open your eyes, sit up straight.
Angels greet you while you wait.
Open the guest book, look for your name.
This is one banquet dinner you wanna make.
Scroll down the pages, name after name.
May I ask, "What did you do in Jesus's name?"
They stammer and stutter, angels start to flutter.
Don't give up yet. Tell me one thing you've done for your king?
Sir, please hurry. The lines are getting longer.
Many phones are ringing everywhere.
Afraid their gonna miss God's biggest dinner party of the year.
End of the year, end of the atmosphere.
Banquets almost ready, would you like to serve?
I can enlist you if you serve the hors d'oeuvres.
I know it's last minute, but if you want in, you serve the food
And make it your win. Put on a uniform, hurry this way,
No time to wait, grab a hot plate.
In eternity, there will be no hate or ill fate.
It's God's first reunion with all children home.
We'll all eat together close to God's throne.
None separated from God's heavenly throne. Roll call is over.
We're all finally home.
"Did you heed your call?"

"Blessed are they that do his commandments, that they may have right to the tree of life, and may enter in through the gates into the city" (Revelation 22:14).

Wooden Park

Take a stroll with me through the wooden park.
Pushing my girls on the swing sets, it's not quite yet dark.
Sliding down the sliding board, dogs waiting for their walk.
Follow across the wooden bridge to the gate that holds their heart.
Take the key and unlock the door opening a whole new floor.
Follow the maze all around, first go up, then go down.
Climb up the pegs to another phase, now take the train.
Looks like a net, maybe a cage. Always in my mind, another memory
    made from time.

> "He will love you, and bless you, and multiply
> you" (Deuteronomy 7:13).

Beach Days

Waves rushing in faster and faster and faster.
Another day passes, thoughts racing backward,
They think they've become my master.
Swirling around in my head, maybe I should have stayed in bed.
As I try to resurface, another thought crashes.
Wow, my mind's really blasted.
As I get up, another one dashes, pushing me down, swirling around,
I'm afraid I'm gonna drown…
Not much breath left underground.
If you could see me now, I almost drowned.
So I started to frown.
Thoughts keep passing faster and faster.

Tears of joy come flowing down. Now I'm safe back on the ground.
God held my hand and always will.
I'm still alive, such a thrill.
Thoughts fading now like waves in the ocean…
Rolling back now deep into the ocean.
God did it again; calmed all the commotion.
Let new thoughts roll into your brain waves.
Making new emotions go deep in your ocean.
Drowning out fear, new thoughts this year.
Push evil away.
Let God keep it at bay.
Be thankful for your life today.
God is on your side, maybe not the tide.
Waves are beautiful to behold; can be dangerous as they roll.
Follow God's lead.
Let him precede.
He's the safest way.
When we trust and obey,
He knows all he will never let you fall.
Unconditional love for everyone
Spurs into a tidal wave,
An ocean of emotion,
God's hovering over us,
Calming all commotion.

> "The Lord is slow to anger, but great is power.
> He has his way in the whirlwind and the storm"
> (Nahum 1:3).

Sand

Like sand slipping through your fingers
And running through your toes,
Washing away all your woes…
So is time ever ringing,
Marches on while you're singing,
Taking my mind captive as the year passes.
Watching it through the hourglasses,
Like grains of sand into ashes.
Sand everywhere straight from the heart.
Shedding my tears, I'm falling apart.
Feeling like I need to play a part.
Meanwhile my heart is tearing apart…
Watching the granules of sand through the glass.
My heart breaking 'cause one's attached…
Some good memories some are sad…
All recollections of a life I once had.
Remember the good memories, remember the bad.
But most of all, be thankful for the family you have.
My children, a reminder of a love we once shared.
Love is like the sand, produces granules everywhere,
All over the land. Love is like the circle of a wedding band.
It never really ends, just circles back to you again…
Memories ingrained in your brain like you're on a timeless train.
Some good, some bad, they cannot fade.
Sometimes make you feel insane.
Love is like time, no matter how it rolls…
Don't let it change your core; there's more to behold.
Worries away, all gone today…
Be at peace with yourself; no need to change.

Let the God who rules the waves
Rule your mind. We must obey.
Peace be still to you and me.

> "For they shall know me from the least of them to the greatest says the Lord; for I forgive their iniquity, and remember their sin no more" (Jeremiah 31:34).

> "I am grateful to God…when I remember you constantly in my prayers day and night" (2 Timothy 1:3).

Roses in Bloom

Pick out a rose beautiful in bloom, watch the petals blossoming to you,
Smell the fragrance beautiful in full bloom,
See the dew on the petals and leaves, jump start the moon,
Then starts the gloom, another cycle begins watering you.
Then one by one, they start to fall. What's old is new in the waterfalls.
Beautiful colors rich and bold,
Fading in time like sea billows roll,
Hear them roar, their time to soar.
Don't wanna leave. Could I stay awhile please?
The thorn pricks my hand, I'm in neverland.
Not ready to leave, I feel a squeeze.
Not ready quite yet, I'm starting to quiver.
I look up; something made me shiver.

I'm not really here. It was all just a dream
About a madman and a terrible scheme.
I'm really not here. It was all just a scam with the use of a videocam.
It's not real. It's neverland where I met an invisible man.
Open your heart. Let love lead the way
To a beautiful palace with your prince on his way.
Don't stare too long. It's a beautiful song. If you linger awhile,
(Uh-oh, hurry) you'll be defiled.
Overlooking the Chesapeake Bay,
The crashing sound is fierce today,
Waves rushing in upon the rocks, knocking off my socks.
The waves could have washed me away, instead they held me at the bay.
As I sit upon the sand, waters rushing through my hands. No more fears,
No more tears, this year. Removing all the pain in your ear.
Do you feel better now? "Wait,"
No time to hate, make a new story, time to set a new date.

> "For I know the thoughts I think towards you
> saith the Lord…thoughts of peace, not of evil to
> give you an expected end" (Jeremiah 29:11).

Cupid's Heart

Although I don't feel the same this year with someone whispering in my ear. The road to recovery. has been long, dark, so is finding a new sweetheart. What I thought would be fun, a new season filled with love. Territory men want to own while I'm looking for a new home. All he wants to do is roam. Get out your bow and arrow, not your time to go. Open up your new heart and give it a jump start. Cupid's looking for a companion whose love never ends. As I date, I learn and grow, rediscover I'm still my own.

> Hands are everywhere, hands in the air,
> Hands up, hands down, hands all around.
> Sometimes it's fun hands, sometimes they're cold,
> But most of all, these hands are growing old.

These hands should tell us where to go, when to stop, what to wear. "Oh my gosh," who knows? Am I inappropriate? Only God knows. Cupid held my heart so tight. He played my strings all through the night. Please don't fight! You can't rush love as we all know. It's not a game like tic-tac-toe. One day you'll win love will bloom again. Meet someone like you who loves more than you do. Cupid's ready to leave dust in the breeze. Your new love is here, never shed a tear. When you don't know which way to go, dial 1-800-cupid-arrow. He'll come to your rescue. He has the key to unlock your heart. Call 1-800-daddy. Fulfill his will. God has your heart, never fear, you're in his hand to fulfill his plan enjoy the next clan. Enjoy the next new year.

> Love you this year, love in your heart, love in the air,
> Love in your ear, love holding your hand, love everywhere.
> Love casts out fear, love never fails, love always rebounds.
> Love cannot hurt you, love always wins.

Cupid's Arrow Continued

"Your love has given me great joy and encouragement" (Philemon 1:7).

"Love one another deeply from the heart" (1 Peter 1:22).

"To give them light that sit in darkness and in the shadow of death, to guide our feet into a way of peace" (Luke 1: 79).

Lilacs

See the lilacs hanging down over the fence,
Draping around, now let's make pretend.
It's midsummer in the southwest.
Open her gate and you'll be quite blessed.
Blossoms everywhere, you opened her garden.
You're in her space, you'll not be forgotten.
Now plant the lavender seeds,
Take them from their beauty,
You see, the best crop is yet to be.
God planted seeds inside of me.
Now God's beauty, and his peace.
Flowing out from inside of me.
A new season for you and me.
A beautiful crop for all to see.
God's backdrop is exclusive, uniting you and me.
God is now very well pleased
With the new crop he sees.

> "Thou art the God that doesn't wonders" (Psalm
> 77:14).

Songbirds

Sing a new song, sing with some cheer.
Hear the cardinals serenade us this year.
Flying around from tree to tree.
Finding new love for you and for me.
Looking for a safe place to nest,
Our new baby birds are next year's guest.
Make sure they're hidden in a tree.
So nothing harms them, and they're free.
Nest is left in sight of prey, can fly in and harm again.
So keep it private and safe from guests,
And then your nest will truly be blessed.

"In his hand is the life of every creature and the
breath of all mankind" (Job 12:10).

Butterfly

I feel the warm touch under my skin.
Spring is here, my season to spin.
Twirl around and play all day,
Spinning around like a toy top today.
Out of cocoon like an empty tomb…
Stop at the water, twirl in the breeze,
Oh my, stay away from the bees on the leaves, please.
Lots of pollen on the trees.
My coiled tongue will be pleased.
Fireflies are out tonight. Think it's time to take my flight.
I dance around like Cinderella,
Twist and turn and still no fella…
"Oh my," it's time to fly,

It's twelve o'clock, and I'm still way up high,
"Uh-oh," time for my show,
No one to wake me up, I'm home alone,
Just a little tickle in my ear…
I think it's an ant doing his dance.
I'm starting to see it at a glance.
Buzzing around, I hear no sound.
Time to eat before I sleep,
I hope no one will peep
Like little bopeep.
I'm just one of God's sheep,
Neverland is where I'll land…

"Let the fields rejoice, and all that is therein" (1 Chronicles 16:32).

Hershey's Kisses

I feel a Hershey's battle every single day.
Every time I wake up, Mr. Hershey's on his way…
An ocean of chocolate coming my way.
Hershey kisses dancing always in array…
Spotlights on there time to play.
So afraid, I'm gonna cave,
One, two, three, four, as soon as my feet hit the floor,
Five, six, seven, eight, dancing solo at my door,
Worried about what snack I can score…
Thought it make the camera leave.
So they would say I'm not a tease.
It started with a little weight,
Opening a floodgate, I know a lot of us can relate…

Can you handle a camera with you on your next date?
Pushing me through a new gate.
Why can't any date weight?
Would you like a gumdrop while you wait?
So frustrated as I scrutinize, "Oh my,"
I need a new dress size.
Shhh…don't let anyone in.
I just can't stop the chocolate binge.
One by one, they dance through my head…
Forcing kisses in my bed,
Melting into a new blend.
Thought he was my friend.
Mr. Hershey insisting I try a new blend.
Time to stop, I can't have one,
Out of control, can no longer run.
I feel Mr. Hershey close on my buns.
Snickerdoodle is my partner on my five-kilometer run…
Looking for a new date, maybe he'll be the one!
Peppermint Patty come here.
It's payday. Don't ya hear the cheers?
Let's pick up the million-dollar bar
That will distinguish us from afar,
Walking down the street with hot dollars in your jar,
Looking in the stream, Swedish fish in my dream.
Pass me the gummi worm,
Let's hook 'em, watch 'em squirm…
Now let's take a stroll, I've almost meet my goal.
Watch the Milky Way and have a couple snickers.
Go home to my sweet tart. I know I'm loved; it's a given…
It's love straight from heaven.

"The cheerful heart has a continued feast" (Proverbs
15:15).

My Family Poems
A Time and a Season

Enjoy your family while we're all here.
Feel the love that we all share.
Life is short, sometimes unexpected.
Love every minute, love every second.
Like clay in the potter's hand,
Mold me into a brand-new man.
My faith is strong as strong can be.
God's tears flowed like a river for thee,
And now, they're following me.
So let the son shine in today,
Give grace and glory and brand-new rays.

Don't let the sun go down on wrath.
Forgive and forget till all wrath is past.

> "To everything there is a time , and a purpose under heaven." (Ecclesiastes 3:1).

Our Family Tree

Look up at the tree; all the branches now are budding.
Each fruit bears a name with some traits from their cousins.
They are ripened to perfection where they all can see.
They gain their sustenance from God and now bow on
their knees.
As the leaves wave, hear all the chatter.
Everyone's home. Let's see what's the matter.
I hear a branch break; I hope it doesn't shatter.
I drop down to see what's really matter.
I open the tree trunk, and everyone scatters.
Something's shaking our tree like it doesn't matter.
Hear the fruit hit the ground; I'm watching them splatter.
One by one, they scream, and we quickly all shatter.

> "But those who wait on the Lord shall renew
> their strength; they shall mount up with wings
> like eagles, they shall run and not be weary, they
> shall walk and not faint" (Isaiah 40:31).

Birds

I flew up the tree; you're following me
I can't fly down; I can't see the ground
Stay here with me; we can live in the tree
Not up or down, just flying around
From limb to limb and leaf to leaf
Dogs at the bottom, barking at me
Now tell me what do you see?
I see our little babies hatching with glee
In their nest, all snugly and free
Our new families rest for you and me.
Now we can all fly from tree to tree.

> "My son, hear the instruction of your father and do
> not forsake the law of your mother" (Proverbs 1:8).

My Mom

You watched me as I grew from child into a woman.
You taught me where to go, what to do, and how to get to heaven.
You told me to put God first in life and look to him in prayer.
He's a faithful Father; he'll send angels unaware.
You wiped away my tears
You picked me up from school. Made my bed and breakfast. Taught me the golden rules.
Couldn't help me with my homework, said you didn't know the answers to the problems.
You've been outta school too long. Told me to wait for daddy; he's so headstrong.
He has the patience of a saint even after working all day long.

Made an after-school snack. Washed our families' clothes. Taught a Bible study, all of the neighbors know. Made dinner every day. Nanny taught me how to pray. To keep us from all doom and gloom. Now I am a mother, and I give my love back to you. I'm proud to pass on what's living inside of me, that's great qualities from you. Such love there is no end; it circles back again to the grandchildren in my fold. Love can't be bought or sold. It's something instilled inside as a child and will carry you until your old. It's something you give away. Please make sure it flows. It's beautiful to watch it all unfold. If not the story dies untold. So release it and be ever bold. Thank you for all the memories I forever hold. The gift's that I love giving comes straight from the heart of you two.

"Children obey your parents in the Lord for this is right" (Ephesians 6:1).

"Honor your father and mother which is the first commandment with promise" (Ephesians 6:2).

"That it may be well with you and you may live long on the earth" (Ephesians 6:3).

"And you Father's, do not provoke your children to wrath, but bring them up in the training and admonition of the Lord" (Ephesians 6:4).

"Charm is deceitful, and beauty is passing, but a woman who fears the Lord she shall be praised. Give her the fruit of her hands, and let her own works praise her in the gates…Train up a child in the way he should go and when he is old he shall not depart from it" (Proverbs 3:30–31).

Brother Is a Friend

A brother is a friend whose friendship cannot end.
Rides out the storms of life.
Gears up to work outside.
No matter the weather conditions, stays right by my side.
You can always call me. I always hear you when you cry.
I'll always come over and play outside. Anytime of day,
Any weather play. Thanks for being there always, taking good care.
Since we were nine, we've always been fine.
Since we were young, we've always had fun…
Stays through good and bad, stays through thick and thin…
Always wants you to win. Though the miles keep us apart,
You have a little piece of my heart.

> "But let all who take refuge in you be glad. Let
> them ever sing for joy" (Psalms 5:11).

My Daughter, Jessica

Just a note for you to say, your first day you made my day, all snow
flurries went away. When I first met you, I smiled away.
A healthy baby girl, all new joy sent my way...
Two weeks before Christmas, a beautiful gift. One we love and cher-
ish made a new Christmas wish list.
Opened you presents, you smiled away.
You were the best Christmas package ever sent my way...delivered
on that day.
You're the sweetest child made a new Christmas wish. God bless your
heart right from the start.
As you grew from child to teen, your sweetness (teen to woman) grew
more keen.
Always did your best, from God, you were blest.
Afraid to let us down, have no fear in the sound. Lots of pop tarts
straight from the heart.
Have no fear here; Jesus is always near...
Such a joy you've been my whole life through. Just wanted to say I
loved taking care of you,
thank you for being you, and the blessings you brought into
my life.
I love you always, Mom.

Thanks be to God for his indescribable gift!
2 Corinthians 9:15.

My Christmas Baby, Heather

God sent me a beautiful angel on that Christmas day.
Wrapped up in a blanket. Noel shall be her name.
Another byrum snowflake warms my heart today.
Glimmering in the snow dust, beautiful new face.
No more snowdrifts or snowflakes. Oh no, not today!
Time to go home now, much Christmas joy sent our way.
God blessed us with a new heart beautiful right from the start.
Don't lose yourself out there in snowbanks that aren't fair.
Buy a four-wheel drive; it will get you through the dusty drive.
To heather love, Mom

> "He will feed his flock like a shepherd; he will
> gather the lamb's with his arm, and carry them
> in his bosom, and gently lead those who are with
> young" (Isaiah 40:11).

To My Girls

Just a thought of you today,
Don't see you often to my dismay.
Just want you to know I miss you though,
You're in my heart, never far apart.
A thought away to ease my day.
Just a note to send your way,
To make you smile, enjoy your day.
To let you know you're on my heart,
I loved you both right from the *start*.

"Behold children are a heritage from the Lord. The fruit of the womb is a reward. Like arrows in the hand of a warrior. So are the children of one's youth. Happy is the man who has his quiver full of them. They shall not be ashamed, but shall speak with their enemies in the gate" (Psalm 127:3–5).

My Daughters

Having you here brings my heart cheer.
Spending time with you takes away the blue.
Seeing you smile makes me go the extra mile.
A little love was given a precious, precious gift,
Born just like a snowflake in a midday drift.
Just like the winter snow dust circling the moon,
Grew up way too fast like snow into a dune.
Riding on a snowmobile,
Dancing with the moon,
God will light the way until it shimmers in the dune.
Keep your eyes on the guide; snow bunnies now all grown.

> "I praise you for I am fearfully and wonderfully made. Wonderful are your works; that I know very well" (Psalm 139:14).

Family Tree

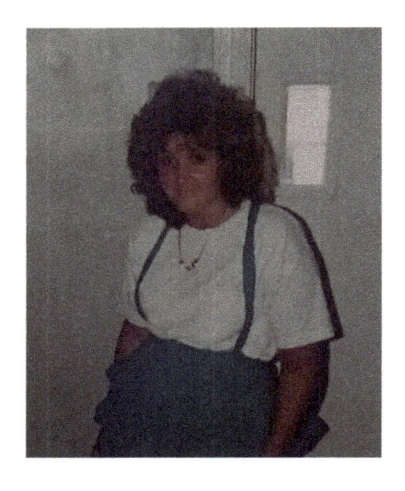

Thankful for my family I still have here with me.
We have a new fruit added on the family tree.
A new son-in-law added with much glee.
Love to watch proud papa's parenting keys.
Take care of my daughter and the rest of your family tree.
Thankful for all of you; no regrets there shall be.
Look to the maker
For all of your needs
Then one day, from heaven, I will watch over there.
Bryant, my son-in-law, love, Mom.

> "Many waters cannot quench love, nor can the floods drown it. If a man would give for love all the wealth of his house, it would be utterly despised" (Song of Solomon 8:7).

A Baby's Breath

A beautiful new face,
Sent here with grace,
An angel from heaven,
Put a smile on God's face,
God's gift of love for you to embrace,
Show her God's love, then she'll win her race.
2 Corinthians 9:15
Thanks be to God for this indescribable gift…

My Grandchildren

God's little design; a new life is here,
Created delightfully sent here with cheer,
Filled with laughter and with tears,
God sent us new joy to get through the year.
God's little angel sent from above,
May he fill your heart with love,
May you bless their father and mother with much love this year.
Keep them safe and guide them throughout their lifelong years!
Giving praise forever, never shedding tears.
Love, Mom Mom.

> "The Lord watch between you and me, when we
> are absent from one another" (Genesis 31:49).

My Granddaughter

A little love sent from above. Can't wait to see
Who you'll become. A gift from God, a joy, a wonder.
I thank God for you now and forever.
Love, Mom Mom.

> "He grants the barren woman a home. Like a joyful mother of children" (Psalm 113:9).

My Grandson

Here comes your son. Can't wait to see how jubilant he will be.
We're all waiting to hold your hand.
To guide you with strength until you're a man.
With a tear in my eye, we usher you in.
God's next surprise, a little man.
Love, Mom Mom.

Thanks be to God for his indescribable gift.
2 Corinthians 9:15

Friends

A friend is someone who's always near.
They'll comfort and console you throughout
Your lifelong years. When I was young and free,
We grew as close as two people could be.
I looked up to you just like an idol.
You were older, more mature, I thought so
Why should I even bother?
I admired your spirit outgoing so unlike me.
I'm quiet, shy, reserved, so I looked up to thee.
Have no fear as we grow older this year.
We're all the best no matter what size dress,
(Size 1 to 99)
The love you gave remains the same.
Though years have passed, I feel the same.
We haven't changed. Year in, year out.
Through the rain, through the stains, my heart made whole.
While tied to a chain…
A friend will always be there any time of day.
You can always call me. I'll come out and play.

"To everything there is a season and a time to
every purpose under heaven" (Ecclesiastes 3:1).

"A man who has friends must himself be friendly"
(Proverbs 18:24).

Friendship

A friendship is a bond which cannot be broken.
Follows throughout the years not with arguments and hollers.
It's a gentle spirit of caring and concern.
One that lifts your spirit up and soars with you through each turn.
It's a kind word, thought, or deed that doesn't involve evil, greed,
Or any unkind deed.
Love will never hurt you; its only here to bear
All of life's little burdens and beautiful thoughts it shares.
It would never leave you desolate down here.
Only wants to prosper you and make new joy to share.

"A friend loveth at all times and a brother is born
for adversity" (Proverbs 17:17).

"In his hand is the life of every creature and the
breath of all mankind" (Job 12:10).

Christmas Joy

It's Christmas day, it's Christmas cheer.
Not many presents to open this year.
Jolly old Saint Nick must be sick.
Hear the reindeer on the roof,
I'm afraid I might go poof.
Hear the clock tick, tick, tock.
Oh my god, it's twelve o'clock.
If Santa doesn't hurry, he won't finish his trip.
Magic of snow dust blowing up in the air,
He's cold, he's shivering, looks quite a scare.
Not much time left to share. Morning smiles
Soon to be shared…

> "Then opening their treasure chests they offered him gifts of gold, frankincense, and myrrh" (Matthew 2:11).

Christmas Cheer

Love you this year just the same as when I buy a thousand trains.
So hang in there, it's a gift of love God sent our heart from up above.
One day, we'll meet him in the air and have a mansion over there.
My faith is the best gift, eternal bliss.
As the holiday approaches, feel the crispness in the air.
When I was a child, I remember running down the stairs.
The anticipation of opening gifts, beautiful music in the air.
The smell of turkey in the oven, the feelings of love being shared.
It's a special time for our family, one filled with prayer.
Before we open gifts, we share much love 'round here.
Gather around the Christmas tree; faces filled with glee
As we hang new ornaments on the Christmas tree…
Time for turkey and dressing desserts beyond belief.
Soon it will be over; our new year will be here.
Let's make it a beautiful blessing. Let God follow through the new year.

"There is no fear in love, but perfect love cast out fear. We love because he first loved us" (1 John 4:18–19).

New Year's Day

Today be as happy, happy can be, today live and love silently.
Whispers of love, echoes of cheer, encouragement in your ear all year.
To grant you and yours a wonderful new year!
I'm slow like a snail waiting for an answer,
Move on, my child, show no fear, just passion.

> The Lord is my shepherd. I shall not want. He maketh me to lie down in green pastures. He leadeth me beside the still waters. He restoreth my soul. He leadeth me in paths of righteousness for his names sake. Yes, though I walk thru the valley of the shadow of death I will fear no evil for thou art with me. Thy rod and thy staff they comfort me. Thou preparest a table before me in the presence of my enemies. Thou anointest my head with oil my cup runneth over. Surely goodness and mercy shall follow me all the days of my life, and I will dwell in the house of the Lord Forever. (Psalm 23:1–6)

Tax Man

When the tax man comes knocking at your door,
Take a peek outside the door because you know he's come for more.
Let's hear one more cheer for the red, white, and blue.
I thought financial freedom awaited you.
My bonus checks $500.00, I only get $250.00. Is it okay if we split
    it fifty-fifty?
Confetti flying everywhere, it's a celebration.
Tax man's got my money, and he's leaving for his vacation.
Maybe I will go next year. What do you do when the tax man comes
    for you?

> But he knowing their hypocrisy said to them why do you test me? Bring me a denarius that I may see it so they brought it and he said to them whose image and inscription is this? They said to him Caesars, and Jesus answered and said to them, render to Caesars the things that are Caesars and to God the things that are God's and they marveled at him. (Mark 12:15–16)

Death Is a Gateway

Death is just a gateway to another land.
It's like opening a door of a grander span where the
Savior gently reaches out his hand and says, "Welcome
Home, child." I've watched you as you ran. I've waited for this
Moment since time began. Just grab ahold of my undying hand.
I will gently lead you to the promised land, peace, solace forever,
Angels dancing there. A beautiful reunion as we gather there.
On the beautiful seashore never more forlorn. Singing with the angels
In bliss forevermore. In our heavenly choir, all worries will be gone.

> "Rejoice with those who rejoice, and weep with
> those who weep" (Romans 12:15).

> "And this is the promise that he hath promised us
> even eternal life" (1 John 2:25).

Peace

As I look back over this day,
All the good and the bad I have, one thing to say…
Be at peace with all men, even those who pretend,
Who try to disrupt, but God's not abrupt.
Be content with all things. Make sure you get your wedding ring.
Peace makes every day good, be thankful and sing.
Godliness with contentment makes you great again.
Takes away the pain, live for today, not yesterday,
Not for tomorrow, just be here today.

> "To give light to those who sit in darkness and the shadow of death. To guide our feet into the way of peace." (Luke 1:79).

> "You will keep him in perfect peace, whose mind is stayed on you because he trusts in you" (Isaiah 26:3).

Retirement

Glad to see you retiring for someone as awesome as you, who's worked
so hard your whole life long through...
As you're growing older living out your golden years...
Just another day of blessings turned into a beautiful new year.
Follow your imagination, fill your heart with cheer,
making new memories beautiful to behold, a new section of life
unfolds. Enjoying great-grand children who are now part of your
fold. It's a gift from God, so no tears will be shed here. We're happy
we have you near.

> "Through wisdom a house is built and by under-
> standing it is established" (Proverbs 24:3).

> "By knowledge the rooms are filled with all pre-
> cious and pleasant riches" (Proverbs 24:4).

Peace Be Still

Whenever you're stressed, remember you're blessed.

Whenever you're worried, pray in a hurry.

Whenever you're discontent, give thanks for something 'cause you know God will bless.

Whenever anxiety rises, run to the one who is higher.

Give him praise, watch your thoughts rise higher.

Peace in the middle of the night, praying always while in flight.

If you feel you're gonna crash get God's gear on really fast.

Just enough strength to get through your day.

Grab your umbrella, be on your way.

Grab your boots and a rainsuit.

Hurry up, follow his rules, run through the puddles, rush through the rain.

God will always bless again.

Don't complain, enjoy the rain, find new things to gain.

Be all here today.

Enjoy all the blessings along the way.

We're on a journey; we're on our way.

To our real home. A heavenly way.

> "For this says the Lord, behold I will extend peace to her like a river, and the glory of the gentiles like a flowing stream. Then you shall feed; on her sides shall you be carried, and be dandled on her knees" (Isaiah 66:12).

This Day

If it were today, I yield it to my father.
I wish it were today walking hand in hand
Many blessings from my father.
If it were today, all clouds would disappear.
I wish it were today sunshine would adhere.
If it were today, all sadness would disappear
I wish it were today all time would disappear.
If it were today, more happy days brought here with cheer.
I wish it were today, new love would reappear.
If it were today, he'd call me his true love.
I wish it were today great things to share in love.
If it were today the end of all creation.
I wish it were today angels standing in my presence.
If it were today, I'd meet the God of love.
I wish it were today, he saturates me with his love.
If it were today, there would be peace on earth.
I wish it were today all prisoners would be lost.

> "This is the day the Lord hath made let us be glad
> and rejoice in it" (Psalm 118:24).

Aged to Perfection

As you look into the mirror, tell me what it is you see?
I see an older version of the who I used to be.
Somebody who looks different is walking next to me.
Holding onto my hand while it's growing old and a little shrively,
A new silhouette of the old me.
Now look into the mirror, tell me what it is you see?
I see fifty, and it's a little creepy. Looks like she put me in the oven,
    wants to bake me.
I see a new heart inside of me pounding relentlessly.
Take your new key, unlock the door to your new floor, where you'll
    be free to be a new reflection of the old me.
Have no fears because Jesus is here.

> "Even to your old age I am he; and even to gray
> hairs. I will carry you. I have made I will bear. Even
> I will carry and will deliver you" (Isaiah 46:4).

Honey Bear

I see a bear, and she's running very swiftly.
While eating lots of honey with many bees chasing me very quickly.
Buzzing around, what's the noise? What's the sound?
Hoovering around more love to be found.
When she stops running away from the sound, takes with her all the
  honey she's found.
Shares it with all the queen bees as they resound.
A little late but more can be found.
Come listen as they hoover around…
Which one to mate with as we go underground,
Where we will escape the sound, twirling around, the sweetest escape
  to her new town.

> "For every beast of the forest is mine; and the
> cattle on a thousand hills. I know all the birds of
> the mountains; and the wild beasts of the field
> are mine" (Psalm 50:10).

The Watching

I'm sitting in a circle in the middle of my room.
I'm completely naked as the men zoom in my room.
Through the camera lens, they think they own my tune.
One by one, they touch my hand, not sure where I'm gonna land.
Vibes I cannot understand rush through my vein to neverland.
Like Peter Pan, I fly away to a place where my soul cannot break.

"All the days ordained for me were written in your
book before they came to be" (Psalms 139:16).

People Pleaser Versus God Pleaser

Let God zoom in your room
When someone yells at you, you look up, but what do you do?
Do you start a fight or, oh no, not tonight?
What would Jesus do if he were next to you?
Are you trying to please man or the one who holds your hand?
God looks down and sees all the messes people leave
And, oh, how we do grieve.
The savior will never betray you.
Wants to help us all the way as we journey throughout the day.
One quick prayer, he's on his way. Angels sent cannot betray.

Follow through, follow through, angels dust turned into dew.
Quick to listen, slow to speak, be like the roadrunner. *Meep, meep!*
Always turn the other cheek.
Don't just sit there and blindly stare.
State your case, share some grace, finish your own race at your own
    pace.
Never let anyone scream in your face.
Tell you you're a disgrace
Or change the pace of your race.
Your opinion matters, hold tightly onto grace, keep your head up,
    and make sure you pray every day.
God will meet you there. No need to be scared.

> "Cast your cares on the Lord, and he will sus-
> tain you. he will never permit the righteous to be
> moved" (Psalm 55:22).

Heart

I feel a little pain in my heart today,
Not sure if I need a jump start.
My thoughts in disarray.
It happens at the craziest times.
My anger arises. Is that a crime when I start to holler?
To state how you feel at the moments surreal.
Feel the purple power lighting up from the chain.
Feel the angry current flowing through my vein.
Can you let it go or will it restrain?
You're carrying God's torch. With it, light our way.
Everyone's behind you, shining in bright array.
Stay on the right path, the calm and peaceful way.
Follow the heart of God so we measure up today.
Keep your thoughts on him, and he'll make a blessed escape.

> "My thoughts are not your thoughts. Nor are your ways my ways, says the Lord. For as the heavens are higher than the earth, so are my ways higher than your ways, and my thoughts than your thoughts" (Isaiah 55:8–9).

My Heart

As I sift through the ashes of what has to be, I see a reflection of
God's love inside me, a whole new world that's now very noisy.
Visions of angels dancing with glee.
As God's word is read as he inspires me.
Don't look back to the way it used to be.
Press ahead, God has bountiful blessings for me.
Heart in my hands taken out by the bay. Harsh words were spoken,
spewed out like the rains.
Hard to retrieve words so always watch what you say.
The best way to start your day is to kneel down and pray.

> "The Lord lives blessed be my rock! Let the God
> of my salvation be exalted" (Psalm 18:46).

Fathers, Love Your Sons

As I look through the looking glass, and it's me I see.
Now an older version of the dad you used to be.
All the things you taught me come to mind with ease.
Some weren't aimed to please.
Some brought me to my knees.
A father like the son, or his son is like the father.
Either way, they come undone.
Following in his footsteps although he doesn't know he's walking in
    his image everytime he brought him low.
Picking up his hammer like his father did,
Looking for approval or at least a grin.
Looking for a hug or maybe just some love instead of just a shrug.
Looking over your shoulder maybe for some strength.
Always getting belittled to this, there is no end.
Look up to your real dad. Abba is his name.
He made us in his image, died to take all shame.
Let him heal your real hurts,
Fears flow just like the waves.
Billows of joy roll in. God hide me in your waves.
Love us as we are, cover all our scars.
Wants to make us new, heal the scars inside that are due.
Wants to sail to another place where there is no disgrace.
Always God's a gentleman waiting at the gate.
Wants to change your fate. Remove all the hate.
Wants to ease your load, can't if it's unknown.
Now a reflection of who you can be all in an attempt to be the best me.

"A father of the fatherless, a defender of widows is God in his holy habitation" (Psalm 68:5).

"Cause me to hear your loving kindness in the morning. For in you I do trust, cause me to know the way in which I should walk, for I lift up my soul to you" (Psalm 143:8).

New Year's 2020

I sprang up to see what was the matter,
Woke up from all of the chatter.
It's 3:00 a.m.; it's witching hour.
I see a ghost, thinks he's my host.
He's waiting to share another toast.
It's New Year's Eve, roll up your sleeves.
Jump outta bed, he cannot leave.
I meet his buddies one by one.
There scared away as I circle the sun,
They zoom on their broom to a new room,
It's 2020. Let's shoot for the moon.
Space invaders need a new tune,
Bright spot when they hit the other side of the moon.
Truth is I think it's just another lunar.
Connect the stars one by one,
Connected to my heart needed a new jump start.

> "When there were no depths I was brought forth, when there were no fountains abounding with water" (Proverbs 8:24).

> "Before the mountains were settled before the hills, I was brought forth" (Proverbs 8:25).

> "When he prepared the heavens I was there" (Proverbs 8:27).

The Forest

Write down your thoughts while tied to the tree.
Gain sustenance from the Lord living through me.
While each branch is freed very carefully
Exposing the roots of the tree naked to see.
While walking through the forest, I feel a little squeeze,
Something brought me to my knees,
It wasn't the trees who were bothering me,
It was a shadow I see in the breeze,
Uh-oh, it's following me!
Suddenly I feel a little weak in the knees.
He's trying to attach himself to me.
Something caught my eye, a silhouette in the sky,
Not sure of its intent knocked me down
And made a dent.
I fell on the ground and hear another sound.

Uh-oh, don't turn around.
Don't stay on the ground. They're dropping bombs around.
It's never a win if you have war within.
I hear the sound. I hear the sound.
Oh my god, I'm on enemies' ground.
Let not the nation drowned,
I see a treehouse; it's all around.
Let's make a run for it, make no sound.
Clear the forest of the trees so we can see, who's attacking me.
In war, there is no win, and no new life will begin.
We need to pray; we need to pray.
For God to give us brighter days.
To end the storm, to end the rain, there's new life to regain.

Refrain, refrain,
So stay in your tree house.
Don't venture out until the sun comes back out.

Watch all emotions flooding back through.
Live out loud your new life make sure to console.
Every branch pruned for the glory of our king.
Stay away from idle chatter and everything that doesn't matter.
Don't let the terrorist win the one residing within.
Start with prayer every day. Let us humbly bow and pray.
He's fighting with you, you're fighting with me,
When will it stop peace needs to be.
There's freedom for you, there's freedom for me, all while the chains
    wrapped tightly around me.
I rejoice with you, you rejoice with me,
Peace from our Father sent to comfort me.

> "Do not be afraid, you beasts of the field; for
> the open pastures are springing up, and the tree
> bears it's fruit; the fig tree and the vine yield their
> strength" (Joel 2:22).

> "So I will restore to you the years that the swarm-
> ing locust has eaten, the crawling locust, the con-
> suming locust, and the chewing locust, my great
> army which I sent amount you" (Joel 25:25).

God's Justice Versus Man's Injustice

When injustice seems to prevail,
Don't fret because they're not placed in jail.
When evil's swirling all around,
Make sure love continues to prevail.
Remember angels unaware don't easily scare.
Guardian angels taking notes instead of pushing actions down our
Throats.
Police writing us up for traffic citations,
Angels trying to help us regain our traction.
Some police officers need forced rotation,
Or off the force or maybe a vacation.
Living life in the fast lane,
Blow by blow, they start to throw firebrands.
You stole my freedom where I stand,
God is still trying to bless our land.
Someone committed a horrible crime,
And we cannot live peacefully now while alive.
Don't harm his prophet for your personal gain.
God isn't playing games in the rain.
Heaven wept at the sound, God said its finished time to receive your
Crown.
Let justice prevail! Please don't derail!

> And there has been no day like that before it or
> after it, that the Lord heeded the voice of a man,
> for the Lord fought for Israel. (Joshua 10:14)

Raindrops

Do you ever wonder what you would feel,
If you could make it rain every time you were afraid?
Do you ever wonder what you would do if you thought everyone was
    against you?
Do you ever wonder how it would be if the rain never stopped even
    when you felt glee?
Each raindrop is a tear shed for a harsh deed someone did this year.
It started with a pond, spiraled into a lake.
Didn't stop there, flowed into the bay,
Made it into the ocean and never allowed to drain.
Each tear never wasted like the salt into the bay. It's a life preserver,
    Throw more of it my way,
    then you're safe to say it's gonna be another wonderful day!

> "When you pass through the waters, I will be with you; and through the rivers, they shall not overflow you. When you walk through the fire, you shall not be burned, nor shall the flame scorch you" (Psalm 43:2).

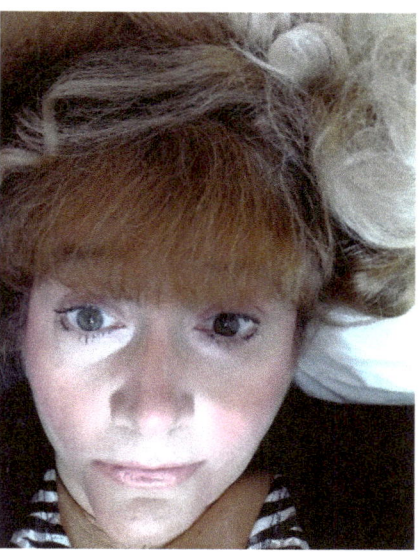

About the Author

Sherri A. Byrum is from Baltimore, Maryland. She is excited to share her emotions in poetic form with you. Also included are some photos from her childhood to adult. It's a joy for her to share the love of God and how he carried her through her tragedy to the writing of *Sunbeam* book. Sherri is thankful for God's love and protection and healing in her life. All of the poems are true and stem from real-life events. She tried to incorporate humorous poems from real-life situations. Sherri's faith is what held her together and carried her here. She would like to share Jeremiah 29:11 with you as one of her favorite scriptures that God assured was a promise to all of his children. God carried her through to write her thoughts down everytime she was upset about a situation in life instead of expressing outward anger. It helped her learn to how to calm down in dramatic crisis scenarios. It was amazing to feel lighthearted and be happy while traveling through a hardship.

Sherri would like to encourage you to cast your cares on God, for he cares for you. (1 Peter 5:7) Be anxious for nothing and thankful for all things. She would like to dedicate this book to her daughters, Jessica Byrum and Heather Byrum-Evans, and two grandchildren, Presley and Easton Evans. She loves them, and couldn't imagine life without them. Sherri hopes everyone can find some humor and healing through some of life's crisis.

May we learn to practice random acts of kindness instead of random acts of violence.

CPSIA information can be obtained
at www.ICGtesting.com
Printed in the USA
BVHW051256240321
603339BV00011BA/1253